I CAN READ ABOUT
PIONEERS

Written by C. J. Naden

Illustrated by Joel Snyder

Troll Associates

A pioneer is someone who goes first.
A pioneer is someone who opens a path
for others to follow.

American pioneers changed the size of the United States.
They settled the land from the Appalachian Mountains in the East
all the way to the Pacific Ocean. They opened new paths
for others to follow.

Many pioneers became famous. Daniel Boone and Davy Crockett are two well-known names.

Most pioneers did not become famous.
But they are the true heroes of the pioneer story.
They helped to make the country grow.

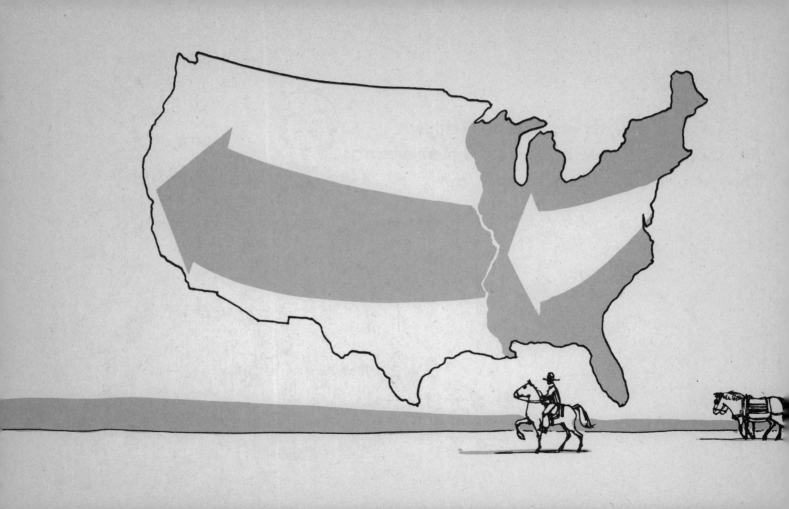

From about 1760 to 1850, pioneers moved westward in two big pushes. After the first push, Americans settled in the Mississippi Valley. After the second push, they reached the West Coast, and the Pacific Ocean.

The pioneers had to be brave
and strong. But they probably did not
think much about bravery. They were too busy thinking
about rich farmland, plenty of open spaces,
and beginning a new life.

Most people were farmers in the early years of America. But they did other things, too. Pioneers had to know how to hunt for food. They had to know how to clear land with an ax and how to build homes. They had to know how to make clothes, how to fix broken plows, and how to build boats.

They had to know what to do when someone was ill. And they had to teach others.

Pioneers did these things for themselves.
There was no one else to do them. There were no towns, no hospitals, no food stores, no schools, and no fix-it shops.
There was just a rich wilderness and Indians.

American Indians were pioneers long before the settlers came. They were the first to roam the prairies and plains of America. They were the first to fish in the clear, fresh streams. They were the first to hunt the wild animals for clothing and food and shelter.

American Indians were the first
to build communities in the rugged
and beautiful wilderness.

Sometimes the Indians and pioneers lived in peace.
But the pioneers often wanted the lands that belonged to the
Indians. Many times pioneers and Indians fought over land.
Each group wanted to protect its own way of life.

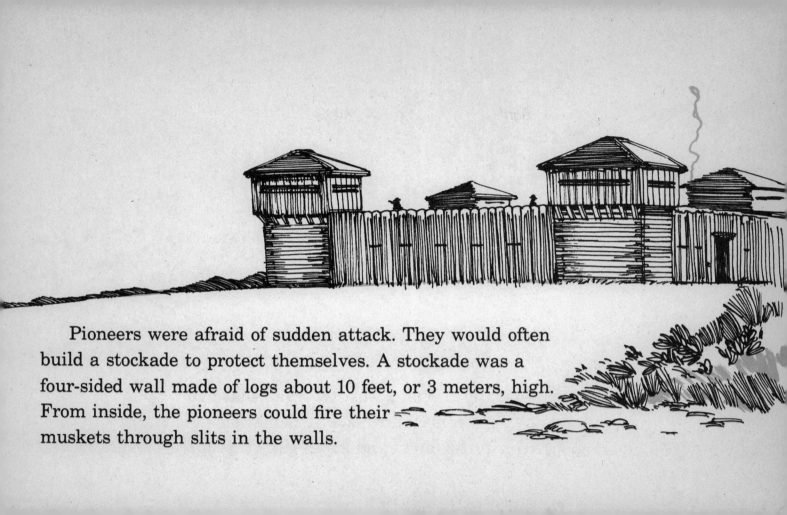

Pioneers were afraid of sudden attack. They would often build a stockade to protect themselves. A stockade was a four-sided wall made of logs about 10 feet, or 3 meters, high. From inside, the pioneers could fire their muskets through slits in the walls.

Pioneers usually traveled west on trails that had
been made by explorers or fur traders. Sometimes the trails
were just paths in the forest and small gaps through a mountain.

The trails were full of bumps and holes and ruts.
They broke the wheels of the wagons. During the rainy
seasons, the trails turned muddy and soggy.

As bad as the trails were, some of the trails had very
colorful names. They had names like the Old Spanish Trail,
the Wilderness Road, the Santa Fe and the Oregon Trails.
And all trails led to new adventure and sometimes danger.

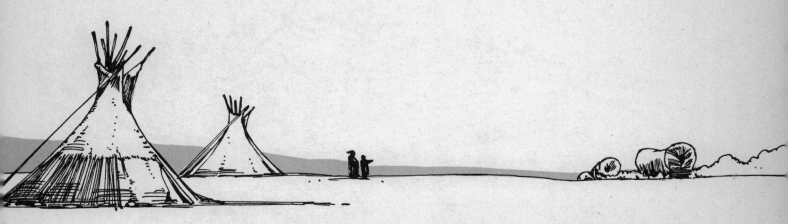

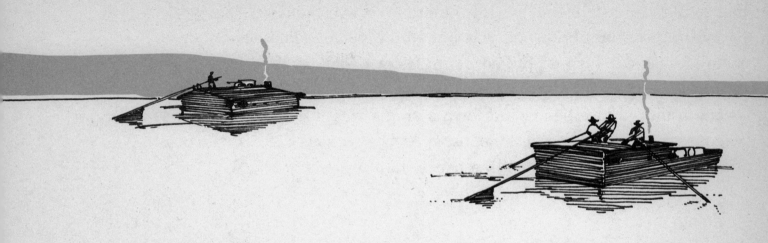

Sometimes the pioneers left the dusty trails and traveled
by water. They built flatboats to cross or float down the Ohio and
Mississippi Rivers.

A pioneer family heading for California had to plan on a trip that would take four or five months. Nearly everything the family owned was put into a wagon. The wagon was covered with canvas and pulled by mules or oxen.

Many pioneer families traveled west together. Sometimes as many as one hundred families would form a single wagon train. These early wagons were called prairie schooners. As the wagons crossed the prairie, they sometimes looked more like boats than wagons.

Not every pioneer had a wagon. Some pioneers rode on horseback. Some even walked for much of the trip.

Every wagon train needed a leader and a guide. The leader was elected, like the mayor of the town, by the pioneers. They agreed to obey his orders. A guide led the wagon train through the wilderness. He had to know the best trails. He had to know where to find fresh water.

Men like Kit Carson
and Jim Bridger
were famous guides.

Wagon trains often met at Independence, Missouri. Then the wagons headed northwest on the Oregon Trail. They went across the flat Great Plains and over the high Rocky Mountains.

Pioneers bound for California left the Oregon Trail at Fort Hall.
Then they followed the California Trail to Sutter's Fort in Sacramento.

The Santa Fe Trail was the southern route that led settlers to the Southwest.

Life on the long trail was very hard and very dangerous. The wagons could move only about 15 to 20 miles, or 24 to 32 kilometers, a day. Supplies often ran out. Wagons broke down. Oxen got sick and died. And people got sick and died, too.

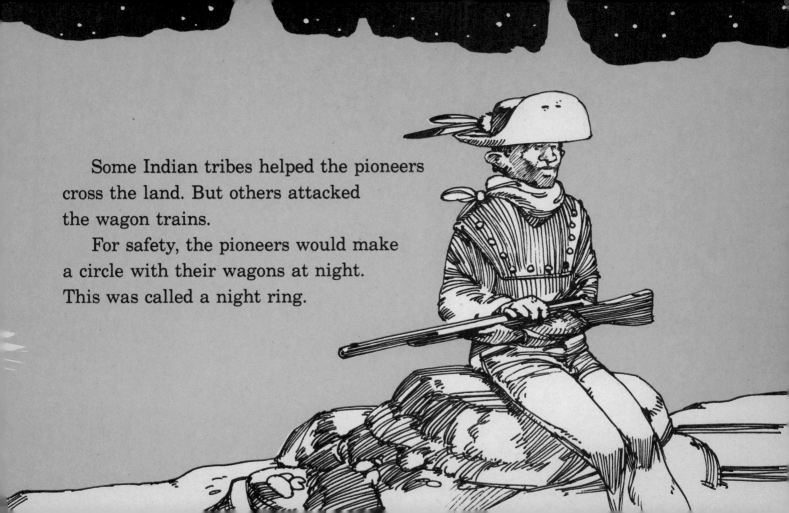

Some Indian tribes helped the pioneers
cross the land. But others attacked
the wagon trains.

For safety, the pioneers would make
a circle with their wagons at night.
This was called a night ring.

Weather was another big worry. If there was too much rain, the wagon wheels sank in the mud. A flood could sweep away everything.

If the weather was too warm, the flies and mosquitoes swarmed about. If it snowed, the entire wagon train might be covered by a blanket of snow.

Most wagon trains left the East in the spring. The pioneers wanted to reach the West before the winter came.

In 1846, a group of pioneers led by George and Jacob Donner were trapped in a terrible snowstorm. For two months they could not leave the Sierra Nevada Mountains in California. When the food ran out, they ate anything they could, even their shoes. Almost half the people died. The place where they were trapped is known as the Donner Pass.

After many long months, the pioneers reached their new homes.
But their troubles were not over. The first thing they had
to do was get the land ready for planting. Planting was even
more important than building a house. Without food, they would
starve.

Men, women, and children helped to clear the land and sow
the seeds. They had no machines, just axes and their bare hands.
Neighbors helped each other with the planting. Helping each
other was part of the *pioneer spirit*.

After the land was cleared, the family could build a house. Many homes were log cabins. The pioneers chopped down trees. They fitted the logs together to make a one-room house. Then they filled the gaps between the logs with mud or moss to keep out the cold and rain. Everybody helped everyone else.

There was a fireplace inside the cabin.
The pioneers made most of their own furniture.
Sometimes a family slept only on piles of quilts. If the cabin had a loft,
the children slept up there. They reached the loft by climbing a steep ladder.

There was much work to be done in the new land. But people also found time for fun. When they could, families would get together for parties. They had corn-husking parties and quilting parties. They ran races and had shooting contests. Soon someone picked up a fiddle, and then the dancing and singing would begin.

The American pioneers kept moving farther and farther
west, making the country bigger and stronger.

Although their life was hard, they had many good things.
They had wide open spaces, rich land,
fresh water and clean air. They had freedom…

...and they had the great pioneer spirit
that helped America grow
into a great nation.